Contents

Cover Design • Temple of Design
Cover Photo • Stockbyte

Order No. 1140b
ISBN No. 1-857200454

Exclusive Distributors:
Walton Manufacturing Co. Ltd.
Unit 6A, Rosemount Park Drive, Rosemount Business Park,
Ballycoolin Road, Blanchardstown, Dublin 15, Ireland

Walton Music Inc.
P.O. Box 874, New York, NY 10009, U.S.A.

Printed in Ireland by ColourBooks Ltd.

3 5 7 9 0 8 6 4 2

Red Is The Rose

Red is the rose by yon-der gar-den grows and fair is the li-ly of the val - - ley, clear is the wa - ter that flows from the Boyne, but my love is fair - er than a - - ny.

'T was down by Killarney's green woods that we strayed
And the moon and the stars they were shining
The moon shone its rays on her locks of golden hair,
And she swore she'd be my love for ever.

Repeat Chorus

It's not for the parting that my sister pains
It's not for the grief of my mother
It is all for the loss of my bonnie Irish lass,
That my heart is breaking for ever.

Repeat Chorus

The Gap of Dunloe, Killarney, Co. Kerry.

Carrickfergus

My childhood days bring back sad reflections of happy times I spent so long ago
My boyhood friends and my own relations have all passed on now like melting snow
But I'll spend my days in endless roaming, soft is the grass, my bed is free
Ah! to be back now in Carrickfergus, on that long road down to the sea.

And in Kilkenny, it is reported, there are marble stones as black as ink
With gold and silver I would support her, but I'll sing no more now till I get a drink
I'm drunk today, and I'm seldom sober, a handsome rover from town to town
Ah! but I'm sick now, my days are numbered, so come all ye young men and lay me down.

Carrickfergus.

Nora

The golden-dewed daffodils shone, Nora; And danced in the breeze on the lea
When I first said I loved only you, Nora; And you said you loved only me.

The birds in the trees sang their songs, Nora; Of happier transports to be
When I first said I loved only you, Nora; And you said you loved only me.

Our hopes they have never come true, Nora; Our dreams they were never to be
Since I first said I loved only you, Nora; And you said you loved only me.

The Bard of Armagh

It was long before the shamrock, dear Isle's lovely emblem
Was crushed in its beauty by the Saxon's lion paw
And all the pretty colleens around me would gather
Call me their bold Phelim Brady, the Bard of Armagh.

How I love to muse on the days of my boyhood
Though four score and three years have fled by them
It's king's sweet reflection that every young joy
For the merry-hearted boys make the best of old men.

At a fair or a wake I would twist my shillelah
And trip through a dance with my brogues tied with straw
There, all the pretty maidens around me gather
Call me their bold Phelim Brady, the Bard of Armagh.

In truth I have wandered this wide world over
Yet Ireland's my home and a dwelling for me
And, oh, let the turf that my old bones shall cover
Be cut from the land that is trod by the free.

And when sergeant death in his cold arms doth embrace
And lull me to sleep with old Erin-go-bragh
By the side of my Kathleen, my dear pride, oh, place me
Then forget Phelim Brady, the Bard of Armagh.

Armagh.

The Nightingale

brave gren - a - dier, and they kissed so sweet and comfor-ting as they clung to each

other _____ They went arm in arm a - long the road like sis - ter and

broth - er. _____ They went arm in arm a - long the road 'till they

came to a stream _____ and they both sat down to -

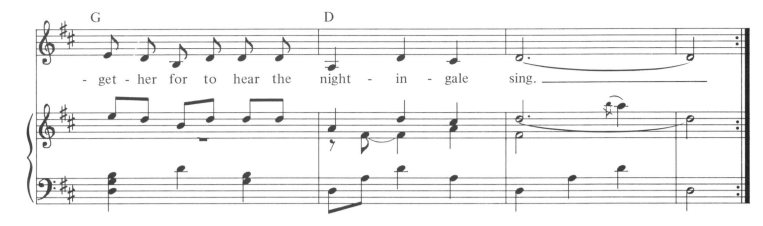

-get - her for to hear the night - in - gale sing. ____

And out of his knapsack he took a fine fiddle
And he played her such a merry tune as you ever did hear
And he played her such a merry tune as the valleys did ring
And they both sat down together for to hear the nightingale sing.

Wishing Chair, Giants Causeway, Co. Antrim.

14

The Wearing Of The Green

Oh Pad - dy dear now did you hear the news that's go - ing round? The Sham-rock is for- -bid by law to grow on Ir - ish ground. No more St. Pat - rick's Day we'll keep, his col - ours can't be seen. For there's a cru - el

law a - gainst the wear - in' of the green.

I met with Napper Tandy and he took me by the hand
And he said, "How's poor old Ireland and how does she stand?"
She's the most distressful country that ever yet was seen
For they're hangin' men an' women for the wearing of the Green.

And if the colour we must wear is England's cruel Red
Let it remind us of the blood that Ireland has shed
Then pull the shamrock from your hat, and throw it on the sod
And never fear, 'twill take root there, tho' under foot 'tis trod.
When the law can stop the blades of grass from growing as they grow
And when the leaves in summer-time, their colour dare not show
Then I will change the colour, too, I wear in my caubeen
But 'till that day, please God, I'll stick to wearing of the Green.

An Eviction scene.

The Meeting Of The Waters

There is not in this wide world a val - ley so sweet as the vale in who-se bo - som the bright wat - ers meet, Oh the last rays o - f feel - ing and life must de - part, ere the bloom of that val - ley shall fade from my

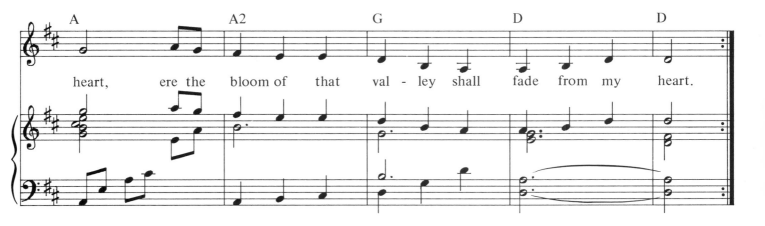

heart, ere the bloom of that val - ley shall fade from my heart.

Yet it was not that nature had shed o'er the scene
Her purest of crystal and brightest of green
'Twas not her soft magic of streamlet or hill
Oh! no — it was something more exquisite still.

'Twas that friends, the beloved of my bosom, were near
Who made every dear scene of enchantment more dear
And who felt how the best charms of Nature improve
When we see them reflected from looks that we love.

Sweet Vale of Avoca! how calm could I rest
In thy bosom of shade, with the friends I love best
Where the storms that we feel in this cold world should cease
And our hearts, like thy waters, be mingled in peace.

Avoca, Co. Wicklow.

The Hills Of Kerry

Chorus:

The pa - lm trees wave on high _____ a - long the fer - tile shore.

A - dieu the Hills of Ker - ry I ne'er will see no more. _____ Oh why did I

The noble and the brave have departed from our shore
They've gone off to a foreign land where the wild canyons roar
No more they'll see the shamrock, the plant so dear to me
Or hear the small birds singing around sweet Tralee.

Repeat Chorus

No more the sun will shine on that blessed harvest morn
Or hear our reaper singing in a golden field of corn
There's a band for every woe and a cure for every pain
But the happiness of my darling girl I never will see again

Repeat Chorus

My Mary Of The Curling Hair

siúl go so-cair a-gus siúl go ciúnn. My love, my pearl my own dear girl, my moun-tain maid a-rise.

A-

(Repeat Chorus after each Verse)

Wake, linnet of the osier grove! Wake, trembling, stainless, virgin dove!
Wake, nestling of a parent's love! Let Moran see thine eyes.

I am no stranger, proud and gay, To win thee from thy home away
And find thee, at some distant day, A theme for wasting sighs.

But we were known from infancy, Thy father's hearth was home to me
No selfish love was mine for thee, Unholy and unwise.

And yet to see what love can do, Though calm my hope has burned and true
My cheek is pale and worn for you, And sunken are mine eyes!

But soon my love shall be my bride, And happy by our own fireside
My veins shall feel the rosy tide, That lingering hope denies.

Peggy Gordon

I'm so in love that I can't deny it; My heart lies smothered in my breast
But it's not for you to let the world know it; A troubled mind can know no rest.

I put my head to a glass of brandy; It was my fancy, I do declare
For when I'm drinking, I'm always thinking; And wishing Peggy Gordon was here.

I wish I was in some lonesome valley; Where womankind cannot be found
Where the little birds sing upon the branches; And every moment a different sound.

Oh Peggy Gordon, you are my darling; Come sit you down upon my knee
And tell to me the very reason; Why I am slighted so by thee.

Do You Want Your Old Lobby Washed Down

Brightly

I've a nice lit-tle cot and a small bit of land and a place by the side of the sea. _____ And I care a-bout no-one be-cause I be-lieve that no-bo-dy cares a-bout me.

My peace is des - troyed and I'm fair - ly a - nnoyed by a lass - ie who works in the town. _____ She sighs ev - 'ry day as she pass - es this way, "Do you want your old lob - by washed down, Con

Chorus:

Do you want your old lob - by washed down,

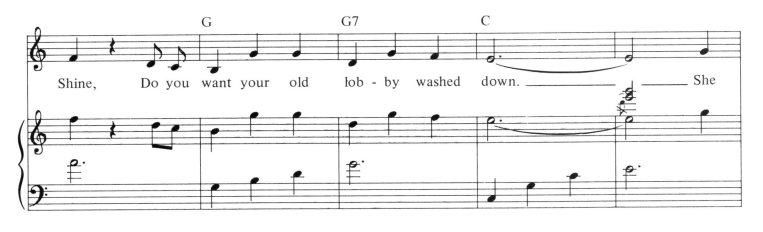

Shine, Do you want your old lob-by washed down. _____ She

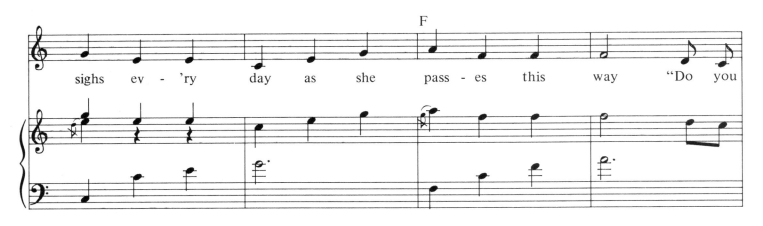

sighs ev - 'ry day as she pass - es this way "Do you

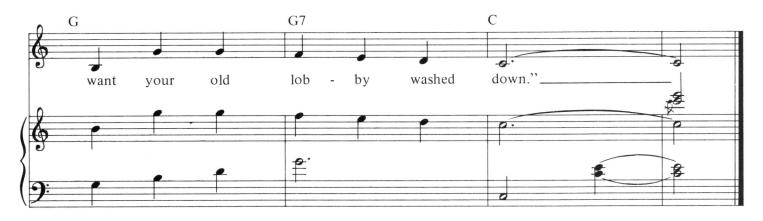

want your old lob - by washed down." _____

The other day the old landlord came by for his rent: I told him no money I had
Besides 'twasn't fair for to ask me to pay: The times were so awfully bad
He felt discontent at not getting his rent; And he shook his big head in a frown
Says he "I'll take half", but says I with a laugh; "Do you want your old lobby washed down".

Repeat Chorus:—

Now the boys look so bashful when they go out courting; They seem to look so very shy
As to kiss a young maid, sure they seem half afraid; But they would if they could on the sly
But me, I do things in a different way; I don't give a nod or a frown
When I goes to court, I says, "here goes for sport"; Do you want your old lobby washed down.

Repeat Chorus:—

Peasants, Queenstown, Co. Cork.

The Wild Colonial Boy

There was a wild col - on - ial boy Jack Dug - gan was his name. _____ He was born and raised in I - re - land in a house called Cast - le - maine. _____ He was his fath - er's

30

At the early age of sixteen years he left his native home
And to Australia's sunny land, he was inclined to roam
He robbed the rich and he helped the poor; He stabbed James MacEvoy
A terror to Australia was, the wild Colonial Boy.

One morning on the prairie, wild Jack Duggan rode along
While listening to the mocking bird, singing a cheerful song
Out jumped three troopers, fierce and grim; Kelly, Davis and Fitzroy
They all set out to capture him, the wild Colonial Boy.

Surrender now, Jack Duggan, come; You see there's three to one
Surrender in the Queen's name, sir; You are a plundering son
Jack drew two pistols from his side; And glared upon Fitzroy
I'll fight, but not surrender, cried the wild Colonial Boy.

He fired a shot at Kelly, which brought him to the ground
He fired point blank at Davis, too, who fell dead at the sound
But a bullet pierced his brave young heart, from the pistol of Fitzroy
And that was how they captured him, the wild Colonial Boy.

The Leaving of Liverpool

I have shipped on a Yankee sailing ship
Davy Crockett is her name
And her Captain's name was Burgess
And they say that she's a floating hell.

Repeat Chorus:—

Oh the sun is on the harbour love
And I wish I could remain
For I know it will be a long, long time
Before I see you again.

Repeat Chorus:—

The Curragh Of Kildare

Oh the win - ter it is passed, and the sum-mer's come at last, And the birds they are sing-ing in the trees. _____ _____ Their lit - tle hearts are glad but mine is ve - ry sad for my true love is far a - way from me. _____

All you that are in love and cannot it remove
I pity all the pain that you endure
For experience let me know that your heart is full of woe
It's a woe that no mortal can endure
And straight I will repair to the Curragh of Kildare
For it's there I'll find tidings of my dear.

A livery I will wear and I'll comb back my hair
And in velvet so green I will appear
And straight I will repair to the Curragh of Kildare
For it's there I'll find tidings of my dear.

Inver Village, Larne, Co. Antrim.

35

The Shores of Amerikay

I'm bid-ding fa-re-well to the land of my youth and the homes I love so well _____ and the moun-tains so grand round my own na-tive land. I'm bid-ding them all fare - well. _____ With an ach - ing he-art I'll

It's not for the want of employment I'm going; It's not for the love of fame
That fortune bright may shine over me; And give me a glorious name
It's not for the want of employment I'm going; O'er the weary and stormy sea
But to seek a home for my own true-love; On the shores of Amerikay.

And when I am bidding my last farewell; The tears like rain will blind
To think of my friends in my own native land; And the home I'm leaving behind
But if I'm to die on a foreign land; And be buried so far away
No fond mother's tears will be shed o'er my grave; On the shores of Amerikay.

The Flower of Sweet Strabane

Gently flowing

If I were King of Ire - land and all things at my will. _____ I'd roam through all cre - at - ions new for - tunes to find still. _____ And the for - tune I would

Her cheeks they are a rosy red, her hair golden brown
And o'er her lilly white shoulders it carelessly falls down
She's one of the loveliest creatures of the whole creation planned
And my heart is captivated by the Flower of sweet Strabane.

If I had you lovely Martha away in Innisowen
Or in some lonesome valley in the wild woods of Tyrone
I would use my whole endeavour and I'd try to work my plan
For to gain my prize and to feast my eyes on the Flower of sweet Strabane.

Oh, I'll go o'er the Lagan down by the steam ships tall
I'm sailing for Amerikay across the briny foam
My boat is bound for Liverpool down by the Isle of Man
So I'll say farewell, God bless you, my Flower of sweet Strabane.

The Galway Shawl

In Or - an - mo - re _____ in the Coun - ty Gal - way _____ one pleas - ant ev - en - ing _____ in the month of May, _____ I spied a dam - sel _____ she was

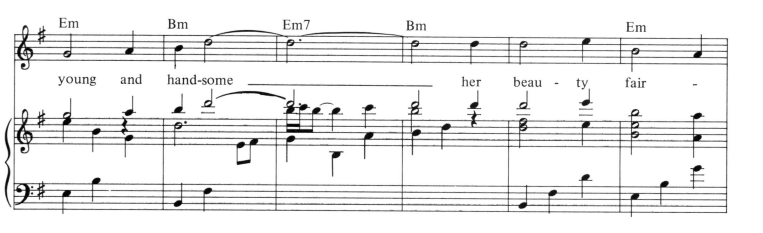

young and hand-some _____ her beau - ty fair -

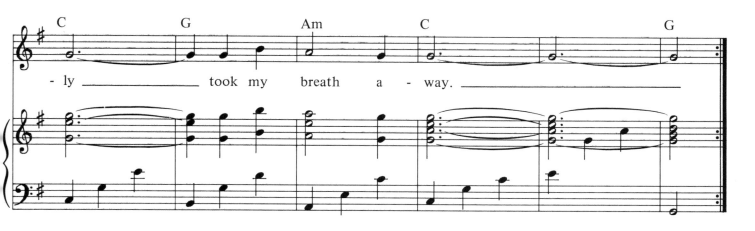

- ly _____ took my breath a - way. _____

Chorus:—

She wore no jewels or costly diamonds
No paint or powder, no none at all
She wore a bonnet with a ribbon on it
And around her shoulder was the Galway shawl.

As we kept on walking, she kept on talking
'Til her father's cottage came into view
Said she "Come in Sir and meet my father
And for to please him play the Foggy Dew"

Repeat Chorus:—

I played the "Blackbird"
  and the "Stack of Barley"
"Rodney's Glory" and the "Foggy Dew"
She sang each note like an Irish linnet
And the tears flowed in her eyes of blue.

Repeat Chorus:—

'T was early, early, in the morning
I hit the road for old Donegal
Said she "Goodbye Sir" as she cried
And my heart remained with
  the Galway shawl.

An Irish Colleen.

41

The West's Awake

Slowly

When all be-side _____ a vig-il keep _____ the West's a-sleep _____ the West's a-sleep. _____ A - las and well _____ may Er - in weep _____ when Con-nacht lies _____ in slum-ber deep _____ there lake and plain ___

That chainless wave and lovely land; Freedom and Nationhood demand
Be sure the great God never planned; For slumb'ring slaves a home so grand
And long a brave and haughty race; Honoured and sentinelled the place
Sing, Oh! not even their sons' disgrace; Can quite destroy their glory's trace.

For often in O'Connor's van; To triumph dashed each Connaught clan
And fleet as dear the Normans ran; Thro' Curlieu's Pass and Ardrahan
And later times saw deeds as brave; And glory guards Clanricarde's grave
Sing, Oh! they died their land to save; At Aughrim's slopes and Shannon's wave.

The Rose Of Mooncoin

Oh how sweet 'tis to roam by the Suir's love - ly stream, and to hear the birds coo neath the morn - ing sun beams. When the thrush and the rob - in their sweet notes en - twine, on the

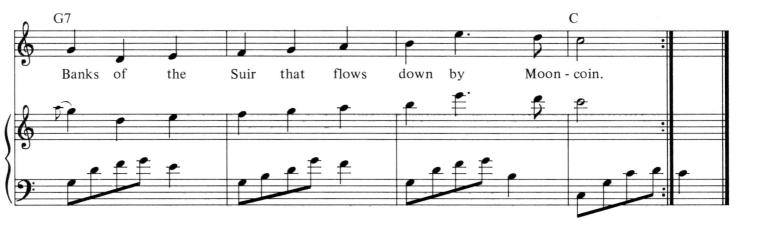

Chorus:—

Flow on lovely river flow gently along
By your waters so sweet,
Sounds the lark's merry song
On your green banks I'll wander
Where first I did join
With you lovely Molly, the Rose of Mooncoin.

Oh! Molly, dear Molly, it breaks my fond heart
To know that we two for ever must part
I'll think of you, Molly, while sun and moon shine
On the banks of the Suir that flows down by Mooncoin.

Repeat Chorus

She has sailed far away o'er the dark rolling foam
Far away from the hills of her dear Irish home
Where the fisherman sports with his small boat and line
On the banks of the Suir that flows down by Mooncoin.

Repeat Chorus

Then here's to the Suir with it's valleys so fair
As oft' times we wandered in the cool morning air
Where the roses are blooming and lilies entwine
On the banks of the Suir that flows down by Mooncoin.

Repeat Chorus

The Foggy Dew

Right proudly high in Dublin Town they flung out the flag of war
'Twas better to die 'neath an Irish sky than at Suvla or Sud El Bar;
And from the plains of Royal Meath strong men came hurrying through
While Britannia's huns with their great big guns, sailed in through the Foggy Dew.

O, the night fell black and the rifles' crack made "Perfidious Abion" reel
'Mid the leaden rail, seven tongues of flame did shine o'er the lines of steel;
By each shining blade, a prayer was said that to Ireland her sons be true
And when morning broke still the war flag shook out its fold in the Foggy Dew.

'Twas England bade our Wild Geese go that small nations might be free
But their lonely graves are by Suvla's waves or the fringe of the Great North Sea
O, had they died by Pearse's side, or had fought with Cathal Brugha
Their names we'd keep where the Fenians sleep, 'neath the shroud of the Foggy Dew.

But the bravest fell, and the requiem bell rang mournfully and clear
For those who died that watertide in the springtime of the year
While the world did gaze, with deep amaze, at those fearless men, but few
Who bore the fight that Freedom's light might shine through the Foggy Dew.

Ah, back through the glen I rode again, and my heart with grief was sore
For I parted then with valiant men whom I never shall see more
But to and fro in my dreams I go and I'd kneel and pray for you
For slavery fled, O glorious dead, when you fell in the Foggy Dew.